Flying Without Wings

Lily West

BookLeaf
Publishing

India | USA | UK

Presentation by *BookLeaf Publishing*

Web: www.bookleafpub.com

E-mail: info@bookleafpub.com

ISBN: 9789360945169

First edition 2024

*Dedicated to my Great Aunt and Uncle.
Thank you for everything.*

ACKNOWLEDGEMENT

This is what I have always wanted to do, what I've always worked for even unconsciously, and I would not have been able to do it without the support of many people. My siblings, Amber and Banana (don't ask, he really likes that name) have helped keep me sane throughout the years, even when they are frankly insufferable. Banana more then Amber, but don't tell them I said that. My friends Jacob Dick, Tiffany Renae, Emi, and Kat have been the biggest motivators and supporters. Frankly it's like having my own personal nerdy cheerleaders. Most of all however, thank you to my teachers. My band director for teaching me confidence and helping me become more of a 'leader'. My high school counselor for always keeping an open door and treating me like a person instead of a list of grades. My horticulture teacher for giving me a safe place to just relax and enjoy being around plants and 'grounding' myself in some soil, some of my favorite poems were written in that class. Of course thank you for my English teachers over the year, especially my Junior and Senior English teacher who helped me organize a whole poetry club to support my love of it. Finally thank you to all my readers! You are steadily making my dream come true.

Keys

Iron, steel, copper, brass.
Click, lock, open, close.
Murmurs, secrets, tears, yells.
Walls, palaces, room, stairs.

Keys.

Twisted metal forming intricate beauty.
Hands shaking as the door opens.
Open the door, unlock what's inside.

What's inside?

Endless spirals of secrets.
Things that make you break.
Give up my key, you don't want it.
Stop unlocking, stop looking.

Mirrors spin and light shine,
stop exposing my shattered glass.
There is nothing here for you.

Iron, steel, copper, brass.
Click, lock, if open then close.
Murmured secrets of tears and yells.

Walled off palaces of rooms and stairs.

Keys.

Feel free to open the iron gate.
Step into my garden of manicured flowers.
Look, don't touch.
My roses have thorns.

Lies, lies, lies, lies.

Walls of lies.
Can't you see?
The portraits lining my palace walls,
the eyes are crossed out,

their mouths are sewn shut!

Damn it, close the fucking door!
Throw away my key!

Stop looking for me!

Run away before they come.
my palace guards will hurt you.
You delicate, delicate, angel.
Run and melt the key!

There is nothing for you here.

Do you really want to see?

Do you really want to see my palace?

the monsters, the poison, the broken windows?
That's all there is!
There's no beauty!

Stop saying there is!

Leave.
Leave before the water boils.
Leave because the food is spoiled.
Leave because the wine is poisoned
Leave because the furniture is dust...

Please leave.
I don't want you to see the shattered remains.
the broken pieces of that used to be a child.
I don't want your pity.
I don't want your keys.
The locks have always been
strong and sturdy.

But your touch makes them rust.

Please don't hate me.
Please don't judge me.

Please forget this perfect palace of pain.
Please forget you met me.
Please forget my key.

There's nothing left of me here.

Dalonia

You are in my web
Full of smoke
and laced with mirrors.

You look at my mask
and find it beautiful,
but you cannot see
the cracks that hide
behind it.

I lead you on,
I let you believe
That I am good
but lies were never built
to last forever.

I tread on a tightrope
as if it is concrete
and I am very balanced.

My mask is getting weaker
its clasps have weakened.
and I fear the fallout
of when it slips.

I wonder if the skies will weep
when I slip off,
or when my mask shatters.

They didn't.
Not a tear was shed
as I fall to my knees
exposed for all to see,
Why are you still here?

You don't actually like me.
I am not someone who deserves affection
or attention
or good things in general.

You must still see this mask
my flaws aren't pretty
My scars aren't attractive.

You must still think
that I am whole.

Angel With A Broken Crown

I sit upon the bathroom counter
staring off
where my mind cannot reach
where my hands cannot feel
where my tongue cannot taste.

and yet I see so much
hear so much.

It's strangely beautiful
the feeling of not being alive.
I find myself lost
in this place that doesn't exist

You can no longer feel it
the chains that wrap
tightly around your ankles and wrists.
You no longer have to feel
that burn in your heart
because you no longer
have a body to carry that burden.

Your memories are gone
both the absurdly happy
and the ones that are so painful

you could no longer close your eyes
without seeing it staring at you
with pitiless mirth.

Or maybe you don't have a reason
for the pain that grips your flesh
and ignites every nerve in your body
with an agony white hot
It burns so much
that you have to convince yourself
that this feeling is pleasure
and not pain
just so you can make it
through the day.

This place is that freedom
that you get while standing at the edge.
That freedom of knowing, finally
that everything is in your hands.

You are in control,
You decide your future.
You decide who you love.
You decide your family.

Or you decide
if terminal velocity
will pull you in
and allow your heavy limbs to rest.

This place twists broken bones
into beautiful wings
like that of God's most
precious and beloved angel.

You decide if the wind
Yanks your arms back
with a sickening crack.

These wings hold a power
robbed from you at birth
and with each flap
You rise higher and higher.

This place holds dreams
that you don't even know you have.

It holds my mind
in a state of not being
so close that I don't realise
that I am shouting, screaming,
"Someone! Please! Help me!"

"Look At me and don't see a child!
Don't see a girl!
Don't see wasted potential
because I have dreams
and by the Gods themselves
I want to fly!"

I sit upon a bathroom counter
and I stare off into
what some might call space.
I find comfort in what isn't there
because I don't want to feel the loneliness
of knowing that I am not alone.

My head turns slowly
to look at the person
that resides in the mirror.
We have been through so much together
and I have forgotten why I ever feared him.

We have sang together.
we have cried together.
He is my beginning
and I am his end.

I wonder if he feels what I feel.
I wonder if he too wants
to pull me in
so we can be together.
So he can cradle my face
against his chest
and tell me that I am not
a monster.

People say demons live in mirrors

but which side of the mirror do they dwell?
I don't think he's a demon
I have seen where he stays
I have lived through his pain.

We are both the
Angel with a Broken Crown.

Fallen Angel

I am a fallen angel.

My wings have faded
to the colour of ash.
My halo has shattered
and scarred my pale flesh
with burns and tears.

I am a fallen angel.
I have left behind grace
and fallen for temptation.
Only to find a world
cold and barren.

So my feathers drop
and my tears freeze.

I am a fallen angel.
My wrists have indents
formed by the heaviest of chains.
My back has seals
formed by the hottest of brands

I am a fallen angel.
I am not good

I am violent
and I am hated.
I am a monster.

I am a fallen angel
I have given up on faith.
I don't know what to do.
I don't know where to go.
I don't know who I am
under all my failures.

I am a fallen angel.
Because there is nothing else
I could possibly be.
When I try to heal,
I only hurt.
When I try to grow
I only crowd.
When I try to speak
I am only wrong.

I am a fallen angel.

A Broken Wristwatch

A drop of water
On shattered glass.

Time is a construct
Fake and yet...
achingly real.

It sleeps on shoulders
pushing down more
than the world ever could.

It comes out as a sob.
Peppermint breath
that stings as it
leaves chapped lips.

It wasn't meant to hurt.
Something so warm...
So gentle.
And yet it shattered me
As I were fine china.

The watch has stopped.
Did I throw in?
Did it simply fall?

It was the hug.
Held for just maybe
A second too long.

It was someone
Who pushed so far
pass boundaries
Made of carefully placed stone.

I find myself hoping
that the wristwatch isn't broken
and yet I can't help but wonder
if the wristwatch is me

And I am broken too.

Lungs

My lungs gained depth
through glass shards
and winding branches.

My heart pumps
thick red sap
tainted with man-made glitter
tearing my veins
with sharpened points.

My throat breaths out
shattered wheezes
leftovers from faded
memories of pain.

Thorned nails rip
at a gaping torso
pulling at vines
that try to sew together
a wound that
cannot be healed.

My eyes roll and bounce
in a head filled with slime
tar, mold, and rot.

My brain slips off
images and words
like melted plastic
drying on a charcoal grill.

My diaphragm pushes up
flesh that does not respond.
Glass pulses with wavering certainty,
flashing memories my slick brain
cannot grasp
as if the shards
are both real yet fake.

I thrust my mangled hand
into the weeping crevice
that is my chest
aching to pull what
shouldn't be there, out.

Stained glass clatters
onto clean tile floor,
splashing blood or sap
I am not aware.

When the glass is out
I stumble to my feet
faintly aware, yet ignoring
the healing pieces of a body

that is not mine.

My eyes roll
And my pupils stare
down a hall
that I'm not quite sure
was there before.
The walls are blank
and decrepit.
torn and ripped
as if the wild animal
I claim my heart to be
has broken free
and destroyed what was once
Unity.

The wallpaper is seeping
and ripped and scarred.
Yet my mind holds only
what may be true
at the end of my journey.

My legs are mechanical
as if they are not my own
dragging me towards a truth
That may be my end.

Perfect glass hands
upon a dead end

taunting me
with a truth
that cannot be real.
The face that stares back
is not mine.

I fear it more
than a mare of night
and yet legs torn from another
force me closer
so that another's bleeding eyes
can stare into mine.

My throat burns and claws
like the fire of a demon
that I have hid for far too long.

The face that stares down mine
is unforgiving while still showing
a mercy I believe to be deceit.

The reflection
that cannot be mine
sways its head
on a broken neck.
Bouncing white strands
over fake features.

Cracks replace their face

where tears have made their tracks.
Tar seeps from where
lines of laughter should be deeply set.
Scaled talons stretch
from crinkled eyes
that hold no warmth
within onyx depths.

Silver ripples across the mirror
matching my shuddered breaths.
The glass melts and mercury
paints my bare feet
scalding me in a pain ice cold.

Am I dead?

You Are Beautiful

The sky in your eyes is clouded
From smokey words
that have seeped into you.

You look in the shattered mirror
and you see the cracks in you that leak blood.
Your lips are scarred
from constant biting.
There are dents in your face
from where your tears have fallen.

You look to the world
to see trees made of
fresh-cut flesh
and rivers run of oil.

You gasp and cough.
As another word slices your neck.
You are drowning in your blood.
In your essence.
You scramble
and claw.
To keep it all in.
But your blood still splashes
onto the burning concrete

that your feet
have melted on slowly.

Till man-made stone
and body
are one.

You fall to your knees
and try to peel your hands
from the sidewalk.
You try to cry and scream
but nothing comes out.

You are scared
even as I walk closer,
completely unbothered by the grill
you have found yourself
kneeling upon.

I pull you up
watching as you stand,
letting my eyes roam.
Over the bruises
and melted flesh
that cover your body.

You look down,
ashamed.
I find myself

wishing for nothing more
then to tear my own eyes
from my skull.
If only to let you hold them
In your melted hands.
To trade your eyes for mine.
So that you may see
The beauty in this dying world.
The same beauty I do

I wish only to rip open
my skin and pour my essence
Into a wine glass.
To hold the crystal cup
to your divine lips.
To watch as your eyes close
and you drink greedily.
trying to pull yourself
out of the grave
you are already buried in.

You give me nothing back
but I don't mind.

You are beautiful.

Porcelain Doll

Fair porcelain
beautiful yet eerie.

No flaws.

The kind of porcelain that glows
under our world's gentle moon.

She moves gracefully
with well oiled hinges,
she dances
she laughs
and the people cheer.

Roses fall to the stage
and the girl's painted lips curve.
She sweeps an arm under her abdomen.
She lowers her torso.

And a rock is thrown.

The doll blinks owlishly.
her pupils now trained on her arm.
Only able to see
Spider webbed cracks

trailing down her porcelain skin.

She blinks again
and the cracks become thorned vines.
Blood curls into the same crimson flower
as the roses that litter her stage.

She continues to dance.
She swirls and twirls.
leaps and flies.
performance after performance.
Until the audience only throws rocks
and her body is made only of thorns
and flowers of blood.

Her aged roses wilt,
dropping petals as she moves.
and yet.
She still dances.

Until finally she stops.

A gentle hand,
warm and alive,
hold onto the performer's
thorny shoulder.
And the stranger smiles.

Tears spring into the doll's eyes.

She had to keep dancing.

She isn't allowed to stop.

But the breathing,
living,
loving person
cradles the doll's cracking face
and pulls it down
till their foreheads touch.

The doll could feel the person's breath,
gentle and consistent
and for once,
she felt something deep within her chest.

Longing

The gentle stranger pulled back,
and the doll tried to chase.
Only to be stopped by a rose,
a single white rose.

and she fell apart.

I'm In Love

I've fallen in love with a memory.
A memory of a girl
That I do not know.

My garden of flowers
Blooms only for her,
And yet I have never seen her eyes

Are they blue?
Like the horizon
Where sky and sea meet?

Are they brown?
Like jasper stones
That line the walls of heaven

Are they green?
Like plushy moss or winding ivy
That comforts you with good luck?

Are they Grey?
Like storm clouds that hold promises
Of rain and freedom?

Or are they hazel?

Like a wondrous mix of everything
A dance you could always get lost in?

My heart rambles for someone
I do not yet know
And yet I can't bear to stop.

I imagine late nights
Listening to each other's breathes
Under the brilliant stars.

I imagine Valentines Day,
Giggles fill the air as I take you
Through my scented garden
If only to give you ever flower
Your heart so desires.

I imagine our wedding,
My eyes softening as
you walk towards me
The music in my ears is faded.
You are the only being in my thoughts.

I imagine peppering you with kisses,
Holding you close as you sleep,
Talking in quiet whispers about everything.

I've fallen in love with a memory.

A memory of a girl
I do not know.

You taint my dreams with wishful thinking.
What's a hopeless romantic to do
When she isn't able to love?

She Walks

Ripples disturb the water
as the girl walks on top.

There is no ice
she is just walking on
a flooring
that isn't there.

When she looks down
there is no end
to the water.
So she looks ahead
to a future
that isn't there.

She's alone
but she isn't lonely.
Apathetic. Maybe.
But not lonely.

She's in a place
she doesn't know
but she is not afraid.
She can not swim
and yet she's calm.

And yet.
She's safe.

She is a numbness
that isn't cold
in a place that is as alive
as a stingray.
As dangerous as one too
if you're in the wrong place
at the wrong time.

The girl thinks
that the place
is more alive
than her.

She also wonders
if she is asleep.
Though time is lost on her
she knows she has
been here for...

Hours?
Days?
Weeks?
Months?
Years?

She doesn't actually know.
She knows in the same way
you would know if green
was yellow
or blue,
without ever knowing
what colour was.

She has been walking
for a long.
Long.
Long.
Time.
and she is exhausted.

She won't show it

Even if there is
no one to judge.
No one to see her.
She will not sleep.
After

Years?
Months?
Weeks?
Days?
Hours?

She sits down
and doesn't sink.
She dips a hand
in surprisingly nice water
and finally she's scared.

Not overwhelmingly scared
but scared enough to
yank her hand from the water.

And she's back to normal.

She vows to never
touch the water again.

She stands.
She breathes.
She walks.

Golden Saint

Gold Glitters across my collarbones
More of a collar than a necklace.
Multiple strands connect at the end.
A tiny bow, delicate in its bond.

My fingers
Small and unassuming
Trail across the jewelry,
Ignoring the coldness
Of that which replicates the sun.

The dress that hangs off my figure
Defines me in such a way
That calls me weak.
Placid.

Behind closed doors my mask slips
I look in the mirror and frown
At a face that retains no match
To the gentle body it resides on.

My hands are careful, soothing
Still
As I peel the smooth metal off my skin.
I do not untie the bow,

Instead I pull it over my head.
The slightest wisp of sound
The only creature in the room.

My eyes are a welcoming grey
As I hold the slip of jewelry.
My shoulders drop
From the ever present tension
That coils through my body like a Python

The dress slips from dainty shoulders
Exposing skin pale as moonlight
Clear as glass and soft as silk

The fabric pools to the floor
As I stare at my reflection.
My body, more curved and subtle
In the absence of my clothing.
Is unblemished,
Pure in its defiance.

I kneel on the carpet.
I let out a shuddering sigh
And fling the now harsh gold
Across my shoulders.

The sharp crack slices through the air
My skin tingles and yet I feel nothing.
My frown turns to a scowl.

I repeat the motion.
It gives me comfort.
The most I have felt
In so. So long.

My eyes flutter close.
My golden lashes caress my cheeks.

I am weak.

Crack.

I am foolish.

Crack.

I am foul.

Crack.

I am corrupted.

Crack.

I am lesser.

Crack.

"Bitch"

Crack.

"Monster"

Crack

"Demon"

Crack

"Attention whore."

Crack.
Crack.
Crack.

Red crosses along my spine
Like cursed wings
Bony and bloody.

My posture falters.

Repentance before a lord
I do not heed.

Love

Do you long for it?

The fire licks up your skin
Like a lover in an intimate embrace.

Will your hand reach out to death
And cup his cheek
As if saying everything
There is to say?

When he leans your hand
Touch starved and deprived.
Do you long to also lean into him
Alone in a void cold and destitute.

Do you long for the fires of hell,
Knowing that the pain is deserved
As you are only the sin
That comes from empathy.

Do you hope
That as he lets you go,
To drift into an existence
That retains nothing at all
That your last moment

Will always be
And always have been
To give and reach out
With the warmth and love
That you yourself were never given.

Ouroboros

I count my blessing
With a gilded silver tongue.

Voids filled tears
Leave milky white eyes.

I start in a run
And end on my knees.
Wind pushes against my form
Yet my body remains in a vacuum.

Who am I to request freedom?
As if I myself am not the cage.
How can I long to fly
When my cracked fingers
Peel off the bloodied feathers
Of my mangled wings.

I am no Icarus.
I have not fallen
After my fingers grazed the sky
And my lips touched the sun.

I fall without having flown.
I trip upwards from the bottom

Clumsy in my grace.

The scent of fresh lilacs
Suffocate me with rot.

Am I not the end
Even as I am the beginning?

Am I not the foundation
As much as I am abolition?

Am I not life
As much as I lead to death?

Does my flesh on which I feast
Do they not count as nutrients?

As my teeth tear through my fingers,
Through my wrist.
Through my tissue and bone
Do I not grow stronger?

I am a god
Forever ruling over ruin.

I am the unity
In what can only be chaos.

Unholy

I find comfort in demons
And safety in sin.

There is fear in what's holy
And trepidation in what's sacred.

My reflection wears large wings
Draped over my back like robes,
Even as honey coated horns
Jut and curl from my skull.

My hands grip the counter
With a creak of bones,
My broken nails dig into fake marble
With the faint smell of blood.

My spine cries in pain
As I stretch abused wings
Its feathers burnt and singed.

My throat is horse as I plead.
As I beg for mercy.

My reflection reaches out,
Cups my face
And smiles in devastating pity.

The Earth and I

The Earth and I are lovers.
Dancing to the same longing tune.
The rain falls on us,
But we don't feel the chill.

The Dirt and I are married,
Between rocks and sand and wood.
We grow mushrooms with decayed love
And flowers with fertile kisses.

Each step is rhythmic
Enticing,
Hypnotic.

We are lovers upon the land.

At night the Earth wraps me
In her warm embrace.
The Winds cannot touch me
Where we sleep.

We step along to a dance
So old and timeless
That even the best historians
Cannot recognize.

The Earth and I are lovers
And when I die,
I will not be afraid
For her love will keep me close
And my grave will carry
The most beautiful of flora

Burn

I had almost forgotten what warmth was.
Amidst raindrops and ice.
I was alone.

Would it have been rude?
To dance so delicately,
Among where I should have died.

Am I dead?

I remember this place,
Yet I feel as if I don't belong.
Like an orphaned child,
Wandering gilded halls
And tiled floors.

Isn't it beautiful?
The mourning of Freedom?

Has the cold come from chains?
Has it come from choice?

Am I doomed to fall?
Even if I have never flown?

Is that a shame?

What would you do as that child?
Would you steal?
Would you cry?

I am numb to the steps of loss,
The shattered bits of memory
That if glued together
Would only display the source
Of my sobbing?

If one eye weeps
And the other stays dry
Does that make me a monster?

I am the plinking notes
Of a piano just out of tune.
I fill halls with beauty that pains you,
I am the tragedy that humans consist of.

I am the empty ballroom of a castle
Long forgotten.

I am the broken chandelier,
That wishes to shine light,
But can only pierce the feet
Of those that wander too close.

When the fire starts
I am grateful.
I am excited.
I am loved by flames.
That kiss my arms and neck.
And I am happy.

Until it burns.

Unworthy

I don't think I would stop it.
The end…
I think I would kneel before it
And simply cry.

Cry because I was never enough.
Cry because I was never worthy.
Cry because it was the only thing
That I could do.

I think I would cry,
Because I know finally
No one would care.

Not that much anyway
They may say they do
But they'll move on.

And you can't tell me I'm wrong
For laying down.
For just taking it.
Because I asked for help
And no one came.

I was loud and frantic

And they just watched.

Apathetic.

Each pen stroke,
Usually enough to bring me even
The faintest amount of joy
Does nothing for me.

The thing is
I think I already died.
I've lost what was most precious
And I continue to lose more.

I am worth nothing but my mind
Nothing but my body
Nothing but my talents.

I am worth nothing but my words.

And yet my mind is fading
My body is unsightly
And my words only bring pain.

I can't work anymore.
I cradle excuses like falling sands
Because what else can I say?
What else would they believe?
The truth that I'm dying?

The truth that I do not care?
The truth that I don't deserve the help I want
Just because I want it.

The truth that I can no longer ask for help
Because it would be seen only as a lie.

I can't even explain the tears anymore
I can't explain anything.

Just that I am dying,
And I am scared that I no longer care.

I am scared that if I met a killer
I wouldn't even try to stop them.

Breathless

I kneel upon a floor
Composed simply of spilled dirt.
My ankles ache
And my legs throb.
But my mind is numb.

My eyes stare
Unfocused and unseeing
Directly at a carpet
Smothered in Earth.

Maybe I should sleep.
Or turn away.
But I am spiraling.

I'm so small,
So so small.
Surrounded by problems
That shouldn't feel as big as they do.

I should have known better
I should have been better.
I should be able to love better.
But I can't.

Because I spiral.

Down down down.
The only grounding thing
The scent of fresh soil.

Wonderful isn't it?
Having no control.
Being abandoned
With nothing to do but kneel
And refuse to cry.

I'm not sure if I can cry anymore.

It hurts to close my eyes.

Prayer

My knees have darkened
A forever bruise,
Immortal in its abuse.

My hands shouldn't be twins
In the way where they have been marked.
The darkness from where fingers dig
Deep into shallow flesh.

Cracks should not line the edges
Of bloodied lips,
Dry from the salt of tears and sweat
Cracked from the exertion of whispering

A plea never answered.

A door locked from the outside
And never opened.

A heart should never fade,
From ignorance and lies.
It should never have given so much
Hoping for something in return.

Maybe God just never heard my cries.

As my back pressed against The Door.
The only thing keeping me away
From the red smoke of anger
That stung my eyes
And filled my nose.

Smothering.

Maybe God just didn't like my prayers
Maybe I didn't thank him enough
For things that I tried desperately
Not to take for granted.

Like food,
However scarce.
And internet,
However numbing.
Like shelter
However suffocating
And happiness
However fleeting.

Maybe I'm a sinner
Never to be redeemed,
Forever trapped in a hell
I was born into.

Give Me Something

Give me the heavens.
Give me the sun,
Blinding and bright.
Give me something intimate
Give me something infinite
In a universe where we are so small.

Give me the heavens,
And I'll give you the Earth.
I'll give you the dirt and sand,
Moss and ferns.
I'll give you the trees that reach
For your touch.

I'll give you the ripples
That move and follow your gaze.
I'll give you every piece of me,
So that when your celestial presence
Consumes what is left of me
I will regret nothing
And I will burn and crumble
Within your supernova.

Just give me something
Something so I don't fade away.

Alone and desperate,
Being destroyed by what I house
On my own.

The Man Who Isn't My Father

I think I watched it happen
That time my mother died
I watched her eyes glaze over
I watched her smile harden.

But at least I knew her.
She was sick for a while,
Fighting against some woman.
A woman who looked just like my mother
But she caught more Flies with honey
But I don't think she ever loved me
Like a mother should.

I never knew my father.
Or well I did.
Just for a little while.
When I was real small
And he would carry me to bed.
He would kiss my forehead goodnight,
And let me sleep in his bed
When I got home from school.
He would let me sit on his lap
As he bounced his leg
And smoked a cigar,

The smoke was always sweet.

I don't know when he left
Or why he never said goodbye.
I don't know why a man replaced him
A man who was so violent and angry.
A man whose every movement screamed,

I don't know when I started hiding.

Hiding from the man who was not my father.
Hiding with my sister
Who quickly sailed to a distant shore.
As long as I was quiet,
She was my sister.
As long as I didn't get carried away
She held me close.
But she couldn't protect me
When she was busy protecting herself.

So I hid with my brother.
We fought often
And I don't remember when I grew fangs
That resembled the man
Who was not my father.
We fought and fought and fought.
But there was comfort in knowing
We wouldn't hold the scars
Against each other.

I don't remember my grandfather.
I don't think I ever had one.
There was just an older man,
Whose eyes were sharp as daggers
Whose hand was quick to inflict
Whose tongue curled around
Vicious words.

The house always shook when he left.

I remember my brother's grandmother.
I remember the way she adored him,
Even as she sat dying.
I wanted to love her.
To prove I was another grandchild worthy
Of the love she showed my brother.
I remember seeing her cloudy eyes
I remember seeing a heavy weight on her.
I remember trying to help.

I remember the way she screamed
When I did.

But my brother could help.
He was always better than I was.
And I remember when she died
I remember looking at her
And wondering who she was.

I remember trying to find memories
Something she could hold onto.
But i could find nothing
So when she died
I didn't cry.

When I left behind
The man who wasn't my father
To take care of the brother
That he adored so much
I thought I was free.
Free of the broken shells
That pierced my feet.
Free of the words
That dressed my skin in slime.
But when I looked into the mirror
I could see him clearly.
The man who wasn't my father.

The slime morphed my teeth into fangs
It morphed my hair into horns,
It sharpened my nails into claws,
It pulled my bones into wings.

And maybe that's why my smiles are closed
Or why my hair is so short
Or why I chew my nails
Or wear oversized clothes.

And when the man came back
I let my guard down
I had let the calluses on my feet fade
And I hated myself for sobbing
When blood followed my wake.

I think my mother finally died
When I lay on the ground,
Fear coating my face
As the man who wasn't my father
Stood tall and proud above me,
His fangs bared for all to see
His hands curled in fists.

I looked at my mother
My eyes pleading for help.
As salt stained my cheeks
I realised she was dead
And another woman had taken her place.
When she looked away
The sorrow on her face must have been fake
Because if it was real
She would have realised that this man
Was NOT MY FATHER
She would have stopped him!
But when I screamed,
Pleaded
For her to call the police
She just looked away.

And I was reminded of each time
I had needed her to stand up for me
And she backed down.
And I was called slurs and sharp words
As the child I should have been
Became some monster.

So I hardened my own eyes
I let my pupils turn to slits
And when I looked towards the man
Who was not… my father,
I kicked out
I thrashed and cried and fought.
When he lunged forward
And pinned me against the bed frame.
When he yelled in my ears
That the police would never help me
That this is a punishment for disobedience.
That because I struck first
I was the monster I saw in the mirror.
And he held me there.
My arm against my back
Straining
With him pushing against me
A rhythm like he was trying to push
Water into my lungs.

And it hurt.

Pain flared and teared.
And I cried.
I cried and sobbed and watched
With gritted teeth as my sheets became wet
With my pain.
He kept pushing and pushing
And telling me he wouldn't stop
Not until I said I yielded.
I looked up
I saw the woman who wasn't my mother
Watching with a determination
Liked she believed that he was right.

And I saw my brother
Horror on his face.
Fear shaking his muscles
And I realised
That while he was older
He was more of a child than me.
And that no one
Would ever
Come to save me.

So I submitted.

I can't remember every sin since then
They blur and ebb and flow.
When CPS came
All professional

And told me it was my fault
And that my father,
As they still saw him as such
Was allowed to discipline me in any way
That he saw fit.

And my shoulders drooped
And my head spun.
And my fangs sunk into my gums.
I was the only one
Able to protect myself.

And I wasn't able to do it.
The first time was a bridge,
But my brother was right there
And I couldn't ruin a child
Like I had been.

The second time,
With my stomach laden in pills
Meant to bring me to sleep.

I had been hungry
And I had fought with the man
Who WASN'T MY FATHER.
And when I fled
He continued to talk
His scarlet tongue
Speaking of his fear

His fear of the monster he saw in me
And I saw in the mirror.

And I couldn't run anymore.

But
And you'll never believe this
It. Didn't. Work.
And though I have people
People who say I was wronged.
I am still the one who must protect myself.
I'm the end.

Despite the distance.
He is still The Man.
And I am still The Beaten Monster.

Where are my wings?

9 789360 945169